Food Hygiene Temperature

Record Log Book

Log Book Number :	....
Log Book Start Date :	....
Log Book End Date :	....

Name	
Address	
Phone	
Email	

TABLE OF CONTENTS

Copyright © 2021 By Design Oec

Title :				
Equipment :		Content :		
Temp. Range :		Location :		

📅 Date	🕐 Time	🌡 Temperature	📝 Notes	Signature

Checked By : .... Approved By : ....

3

Title :				
Equipment :		Content :		
Temp. Range :		Location :		

📅 Date	🕐 Time	🌡 Temperature	✍ Notes	Signature

Checked By : .... Approved By : ....

Title :				
Equipment :		Content :		
Temp. Range :		Location :		

📅 Date	🕐 Time	🌡 Temperature	✍ Notes	Signature

Checked By : _____   Approved By : _____

Title :				
Equipment :			Content :	
Temp. Range :			Location :	

📅 Date	🕐 Time	🌡️ Temperature	☑️ Notes	Signature

Checked By : .... 6 Approved By : ....

Title :				
Equipment :			Content :	
Temp. Range :			Location :	

📅 Date	🕐 Time	🌡 Temperature	✍ Notes	Signature

Checked By : .... 7 Approved By : ....

Title :			
Equipment :		Content :	
Temp. Range :		Location :	

🗓 Date	🕗 Time	🌡 Temperature	✍ Notes	Signature

Checked By : ....   Approved By : ....

Title :				
Equipment :		Content :		
Temp. Range :		Location :		

📅 Date	🕐 Time	🌡 Temperature	📝 Notes	Signature

Checked By : ------------------------------- Approved By : -------------------------------

Title :				
Equipment :		Content :		
Temp. Range :		Location :		

📅 Date	🕐 Time	🌡 Temperature	✍ Notes	Signature

Checked By : ---------------------------- Approved By : ----------------------------

Title :				
Equipment :			Content :	
Temp. Range :			Location :	

📅 Date	🕐 Time	🌡️ Temperature	✏️ Notes	Signature

Checked By : .... Approved By : ....

Title :				
Equipment :		Content :		
Temp. Range :		Location :		

📅 Date	🕐 Time	🌡 Temperature	✍ Notes	Signature

Checked By : .... Approved By : ....

Title :				
Equipment :			Content :	
Temp. Range :			Location :	

📅 Date	🕐 Time	🌡 Temperature	✏ Notes	Signature

Checked By : .... Approved By : ....

Title :				
Equipment :		Content :		
Temp. Range :		Location :		

📅 Date	🕐 Time	🌡 Temperature	✍ Notes	Signature

Checked By : ------------------------------ Approved By : ------------------------------

Title :				
Equipment :			Content :	
Temp. Range :			Location :	

📅 Date	🕐 Time	🌡 Temperature	✍ Notes	Signature

Checked By : ------------------------------ Approved By : ------------------------------

Title :				
Equipment :			Content :	
Temp. Range :			Location :	

📅 Date	🕐 Time	🌡️ Temperature	✍️ Notes	Signature

Checked By : ....   Approved By : ....

Title :					
Equipment :			Content :		
Temp. Range :			Location :		

📅 Date	🕐 Time	🌡 Temperature	📝 Notes	Signature

Checked By : ....   Approved By : ....

Title :

Equipment :	Content :
Temp. Range :	Location :

📅 Date	🕐 Time	🌡 Temperature	✍ Notes	Signature

Checked By : ....   Approved By : ....

Title :				
Equipment :		**Content :**		
Temp. Range :		**Location :**		

📅 Date	🕐 Time	🌡 Temperature	📝 Notes	Signature

Checked By : ....   Approved By : ....

Title :				
Equipment :			Content :	
Temp. Range :			Location :	

📅 Date	🕐 Time	🌡 Temperature	✍ Notes	Signature

Checked By : .... Approved By : ....

Title :				
Equipment :		Content :		
Temp. Range :		Location :		

📅 Date	🕐 Time	🌡️ Temperature	📝 Notes	Signature

Checked By : .... Approved By : ....

Title :				
Equipment :		Content :		
Temp. Range :		Location :		

📅 Date	🕐 Time	🌡 Temperature	📝 Notes	Signature

Checked By : ------------------------------   Approved By : ------------------------------

Title :				
Equipment :			Content :	
Temp. Range :			Location :	

📅 Date	🕐 Time	🌡 Temperature	📝 Notes	Signature

Checked By : ---------------------------------- 23 Approved By : ------------------------------

Title :				
Equipment :			Content :	
Temp. Range :			Location :	

📅 Date	🕐 Time	🌡 Temperature	✍ Notes	Signature

Checked By : ------------------------------ Approved By : ------------------------------

Title :	
Equipment :	Content :
Temp. Range :	Location :

📅 Date	🕐 Time	🌡 Temperature	📝 Notes	Signature

Checked By : ------------------------------- Approved By : -------------------------------

Title :	
Equipment :	Content :
Temp. Range :	Location :

📅 Date	🕐 Time	🌡️ Temperature	📝 Notes	Signature

Checked By : .... Approved By : ....

Title :				
Equipment :			Content :	
Temp. Range :			Location :	

📅 Date	🕐 Time	🌡 Temperature	📝 Notes	Signature

Checked By : .... Approved By : ....

Title :				
Equipment :			Content :	
Temp. Range :			Location :	

📅 Date	🕐 Time	🌡 Temperature	✍ Notes	Signature

Checked By : .... Approved By : ....

Title :				
Equipment :		Content :		
Temp. Range :		Location :		

📅 Date	🕐 Time	🌡 Temperature	📝 Notes	Signature

Checked By : .... Approved By : ....

Title :				
Equipment :		Content :		
Temp. Range :		Location :		

📅 Date	🕐 Time	🌡️ Temperature	✍️ Notes	Signature

Title :				
Equipment :		Content :		
Temp. Range :		Location :		

📅 Date	🕐 Time	🌡️ Temperature	📝 Notes	Signature

Checked By : .... Approved By : ....

Title :				
Equipment :		Content :		
Temp. Range :		Location :		

📅 Date	🕐 Time	🌡 Temperature	✍ Notes	Signature

Checked By : .... Approved By : ....

Title :				
Equipment :			Content :	
Temp. Range :			Location :	

📅 Date	🕐 Time	🌡️ Temperature	✍️ Notes	Signature

Checked By : .... Approved By : ....

Title :				
Equipment :		Content :		
Temp. Range :		Location :		

📅 Date	🕐 Time	🌡️ Temperature	✍️ Notes	Signature

Checked By : .... Approved By : ....

Title :				
Equipment :		Content :		
Temp. Range :		Location :		

📅 Date	🕐 Time	🌡 Temperature	✍ Notes	Signature

Checked By : .... Approved By : ....

Title :				
Equipment :		Content :		
Temp. Range :		Location :		

📅 Date	🕐 Time	🌡 Temperature	✍ Notes	Signature

Checked By : .... Approved By : ....

Title :	
Equipment :	Content :
Temp. Range :	Location :

📅 Date	🕐 Time	🌡️ Temperature	📝 Notes	Signature

Checked By : .... Approved By : ....

Title :				
Equipment :			Content :	
Temp. Range :			Location :	

📅 Date	🕐 Time	🌡️ Temperature	✍️ Notes	Signature

Checked By : ------------------------------ Approved By : ------------------------------

Title :				
Equipment :		Content :		
Temp. Range :		Location :		

📅 Date	🕐 Time	🌡️ Temperature	✍️ Notes	Signature

Checked By : -------------------------------- Approved By : --------------------------------

Title :				
Equipment :		Content :		
Temp. Range :		Location :		

📅 Date	🕐 Time	🌡 Temperature	✍ Notes	Signature

Checked By : .... Approved By : ....

Title :				
Equipment :			Content :	
Temp. Range :			Location :	

📅 Date	🕐 Time	🌡 Temperature	📝 Notes	Signature

Checked By : .... Approved By : ....

Title :				
Equipment :		Content :		
Temp. Range :		Location :		

📅 Date	🕐 Time	🌡 Temperature	✍ Notes	Signature

Checked By : ------------------------------ Approved By : ------------------------------

Kitchen Cleaning

Date		Day		Time	
Building			Location		
Cleaned By			Signature		
Notes					

Date		Day		Time	
Building			Location		
Cleaned By			Signature		
Notes					

Date		Day		Time	
Building			Location		
Cleaned By			Signature		
Notes					

Date		Day		Time	
Building			Location		
Cleaned By			Signature		
Notes					

Date		Day		Time	
Building			Location		
Cleaned By			Signature		
Notes					

Date		Day		Time	
Building			Location		
Cleaned By			Signature		
Notes					

Date		Day		Time	
Building			Location		
Cleaned By			Signature		
Notes					

Date		Day		Time	
Building			Location		
Cleaned By			Signature		
Notes					

Date		Day		Time	
Building			Location		
Cleaned By			Signature		
Notes					

Date		Day		Time	
Building			Location		
Cleaned By			Signature		
Notes					

Date		Day		Time	
Building			Location		
Cleaned By			Signature		
Notes					

Date		Day		Time	
Building			Location		
Cleaned By			Signature		
Notes					

Date		Day		Time	
Building			Location		
Cleaned By			Signature		
Notes					

Date		Day		Time	
Building			Location		
Cleaned By			Signature		
Notes					

Date		Day		Time	
Building			Location		
Cleaned By			Signature		
Notes					

Date		Day		Time	
Building			Location		
Cleaned By			Signature		
Notes					

Date		Day		Time	
Building			Location		
Cleaned By			Signature		
Notes					

Date		Day		Time	
Building			Location		
Cleaned By			Signature		
Notes					

Date		Day		Time	
Building			Location		
Cleaned By			Signature		
Notes					

Date		Day		Time	
Building			Location		
Cleaned By			Signature		
Notes					

Date		Day		Time	
Building			Location		
Cleaned By			Signature		
Notes					

Date		Day		Time	
Building			Location		
Cleaned By			Signature		
Notes					

Date		Day		Time	
Building			Location		
Cleaned By			Signature		
Notes					

Date		Day		Time	
Building			Location		
Cleaned By			Signature		
Notes					

Date		Day		Time	
Building			Location		
Cleaned By			Signature		
Notes					

Date		Day		Time	
Building			Location		
Cleaned By			Signature		
Notes					

Date		Day		Time	
Building			Location		
Cleaned By			Signature		
Notes					

Date		Day		Time	
Building			Location		
Cleaned By			Signature		
Notes					

Date		Day		Time	
Building			Location		
Cleaned By			Signature		
Notes					

Date		Day		Time	
Building			Location		
Cleaned By			Signature		
Notes					

Date		Day		Time	
Building			Location		
Cleaned By			Signature		
Notes					

Date		Day		Time	
Building			Location		
Cleaned By			Signature		
Notes					

Date		Day		Time	
Building			Location		
Cleaned By			Signature		
Notes					

Date		Day		Time	
Building			Location		
Cleaned By			Signature		
Notes					

Date		Day		Time	
Building			Location		
Cleaned By			Signature		
Notes					

Date		Day		Time	
Building			Location		
Cleaned By			Signature		
Notes					

Date		Day		Time	
Building			Location		
Cleaned By			Signature		
Notes					

Date		Day		Time	
Building			Location		
Cleaned By			Signature		
Notes					

Date		Day		Time	
Building			Location		
Cleaned By			Signature		
Notes					

Date		Day		Time	
Building			Location		
Cleaned By			Signature		
Notes					

Date		Day		Time	
Building			Location		
Cleaned By			Signature		
Notes					

Date		Day		Time	
Building			Location		
Cleaned By			Signature		
Notes					

Date		Day		Time	
Building			Location		
Cleaned By			Signature		
Notes					

Date		Day		Time	
Building			Location		
Cleaned By			Signature		
Notes					

Date		Day		Time	
Building			Location		
Cleaned By			Signature		
Notes					

Date		Day		Time	
Building			Location		
Cleaned By			Signature		
Notes					

Date		Day		Time	
Building			Location		
Cleaned By			Signature		
Notes					

Date		Day		Time	
Building			Location		
Cleaned By			Signature		
Notes					

Date		Day		Time	
Building			Location		
Cleaned By			Signature		
Notes					

Date		Day		Time	
Building			Location		
Cleaned By			Signature		
Notes					

Date		Day		Time	
Building			Location		
Cleaned By			Signature		
Notes					

Date		Day		Time	
Building			Location		
Cleaned By			Signature		
Notes					

Date		Day		Time	
Building			Location		
Cleaned By			Signature		
Notes					

Date		Day		Time	
Building			Location		
Cleaned By			Signature		
Notes					

Date		Day		Time	
Building			Location		
Cleaned By			Signature		
Notes					

Date		Day		Time	
Building			Location		
Cleaned By			Signature		
Notes					

Date		Day		Time	
Building			Location		
Cleaned By			Signature		
Notes					

Date		Day		Time	
Building			Location		
Cleaned By			Signature		
Notes					

Date		Day		Time	
Building			Location		
Cleaned By			Signature		
Notes					

Date		Day		Time	
Building			Location		
Cleaned By			Signature		
Notes					

Date		Day		Time	
Building			Location		
Cleaned By			Signature		
Notes					

Date		Day		Time	
Building			Location		
Cleaned By			Signature		
Notes					

Date		Day		Time	
Building			Location		
Cleaned By			Signature		
Notes					

Date		Day		Time	
Building			Location		
Cleaned By			Signature		
Notes					

Date		Day		Time	
Building			Location		
Cleaned By			Signature		
Notes					

Date		Day		Time	
Building			Location		
Cleaned By			Signature		
Notes					

Date		Day		Time	
Building			Location		
Cleaned By			Signature		
Notes					

Date		Day		Time	
Building			Location		
Cleaned By			Signature		
Notes					

Date		Day		Time	
Building			Location		
Cleaned By			Signature		
Notes					

Date		Day		Time	
Building			Location		
Cleaned By			Signature		
Notes					

Date		Day		Time	
Building			Location		
Cleaned By			Signature		
Notes					

Date		Day		Time	
Building			Location		
Cleaned By			Signature		
Notes					

Date		Day		Time	
Building		Location			
Cleaned By		Signature			
Notes					

Date		Day		Time	
Building		Location			
Cleaned By		Signature			
Notes					

Date		Day		Time	
Building		Location			
Cleaned By		Signature			
Notes					

Date		Day		Time	
Building		Location			
Cleaned By		Signature			
Notes					

Date		Day		Time	
Building		Location			
Cleaned By		Signature			
Notes					

Date		Day		Time	
Building		Location			
Cleaned By		Signature			
Notes					

Date		Day		Time	
Building		Location			
Cleaned By		Signature			
Notes					

Date		Day		Time	
Building		Location			
Cleaned By		Signature			
Notes					

Date		Day		Time	
Building		Location			
Cleaned By		Signature			
Notes					

Date		Day		Time	
Building		Location			
Cleaned By		Signature			
Notes					

Date		Day		Time	
Building		Location			
Cleaned By		Signature			
Notes					

Date		Day		Time	
Building		Location			
Cleaned By		Signature			
Notes					

Date		Day		Time	
Building			Location		
Cleaned By			Signature		
Notes					

Date		Day		Time	
Building			Location		
Cleaned By			Signature		
Notes					

Date		Day		Time	
Building			Location		
Cleaned By			Signature		
Notes					

Date		Day		Time	
Building			Location		
Cleaned By			Signature		
Notes					

Date		Day		Time	
Building			Location		
Cleaned By			Signature		
Notes					

Date		Day		Time	
Building			Location		
Cleaned By			Signature		
Notes					

Date		Day		Time	
Building			Location		
Cleaned By			Signature		
Notes					

Date		Day		Time	
Building			Location		
Cleaned By			Signature		
Notes					

Date		Day		Time	
Building			Location		
Cleaned By			Signature		
Notes					

Date		Day		Time	
Building			Location		
Cleaned By			Signature		
Notes					

Date		Day		Time	
Building			Location		
Cleaned By			Signature		
Notes					

Date		Day		Time	
Building			Location		
Cleaned By			Signature		
Notes					

Date		Day		Time	
Building			Location		
Cleaned By			Signature		
Notes					

Date		Day		Time	
Building			Location		
Cleaned By			Signature		
Notes					

Date		Day		Time	
Building			Location		
Cleaned By			Signature		
Notes					

Date		Day		Time	
Building			Location		
Cleaned By			Signature		
Notes					

Date		Day		Time	
Building			Location		
Cleaned By			Signature		
Notes					

Date		Day		Time	
Building			Location		
Cleaned By			Signature		
Notes					

Date		Day		Time	
Building			Location		
Cleaned By			Signature		
Notes					

Date		Day		Time	
Building			Location		
Cleaned By			Signature		
Notes					

Date		Day		Time	
Building			Location		
Cleaned By			Signature		
Notes					

Date		Day		Time	
Building			Location		
Cleaned By			Signature		
Notes					

Date		Day		Time	
Building			Location		
Cleaned By			Signature		
Notes					

Date		Day		Time	
Building			Location		
Cleaned By			Signature		
Notes					

Date		Day		Time	
Building			Location		
Cleaned By			Signature		
Notes					

Date		Day		Time	
Building			Location		
Cleaned By			Signature		
Notes					

Date		Day		Time	
Building			Location		
Cleaned By			Signature		
Notes					

Date		Day		Time	
Building			Location		
Cleaned By			Signature		
Notes					

Date		Day		Time	
Building			Location		
Cleaned By			Signature		
Notes					

Date		Day		Time	
Building			Location		
Cleaned By			Signature		
Notes					

Date		Day		Time	
Building			Location		
Cleaned By			Signature		
Notes					

Date		Day		Time	
Building			Location		
Cleaned By			Signature		
Notes					

Date		Day		Time	
Building			Location		
Cleaned By			Signature		
Notes					

Date		Day		Time	
Building			Location		
Cleaned By			Signature		
Notes					

Date		Day		Time	
Building			Location		
Cleaned By			Signature		
Notes					

Date		Day		Time	
Building			Location		
Cleaned By			Signature		
Notes					

Date		Day		Time	
Building			Location		
Cleaned By			Signature		
Notes					

Date		Day		Time	
Building			Location		
Cleaned By			Signature		
Notes					

Date		Day		Time	
Building			Location		
Cleaned By			Signature		
Notes					

Date		Day		Time	
Building			Location		
Cleaned By			Signature		
Notes					

Date		Day		Time	
Building			Location		
Cleaned By			Signature		
Notes					

Date		Day		Time	
Building			Location		
Cleaned By			Signature		
Notes					

Date		Day		Time	
Building			Location		
Cleaned By			Signature		
Notes					

Date		Day		Time	
Building			Location		
Cleaned By			Signature		
Notes					

Date		Day		Time	
Building			Location		
Cleaned By			Signature		
Notes					

Date		Day		Time	
Building			Location		
Cleaned By			Signature		
Notes					

Date		Day		Time	
Building			Location		
Cleaned By			Signature		
Notes					

Date		Day		Time	
Building			Location		
Cleaned By			Signature		
Notes					

Date		Day		Time	
Building			Location		
Cleaned By			Signature		
Notes					

Date		Day		Time	
Building			Location		
Cleaned By			Signature		
Notes					

Date		Day		Time	
Building			Location		
Cleaned By			Signature		
Notes					

Date		Day		Time	
Building			Location		
Cleaned By			Signature		
Notes					

Date		Day		Time	
Building			Location		
Cleaned By			Signature		
Notes					

Date		Day		Time	
Building			Location		
Cleaned By			Signature		
Notes					

Date		Day		Time	
Building			Location		
Cleaned By			Signature		
Notes					

Date		Day		Time	
Building			Location		
Cleaned By			Signature		
Notes					

Date		Day		Time	
Building			Location		
Cleaned By			Signature		
Notes					

Date		Day		Time	
Building			Location		
Cleaned By			Signature		
Notes					

Date		Day		Time	
Building			Location		
Cleaned By			Signature		
Notes					

Date		Day		Time	
Building			Location		
Cleaned By			Signature		
Notes					

Date		Day		Time	
Building			Location		
Cleaned By			Signature		
Notes					

Date		Day		Time	
Building			Location		
Cleaned By			Signature		
Notes					

Date		Day		Time	
Building			Location		
Cleaned By			Signature		
Notes					

Date		Day		Time	
Building			Location		
Cleaned By			Signature		
Notes					

Date		Day		Time	
Building			Location		
Cleaned By			Signature		
Notes					

Date		Day		Time	
Building			Location		
Cleaned By			Signature		
Notes					

Date		Day		Time	
Building			Location		
Cleaned By			Signature		
Notes					

Date		Day		Time	
Building			Location		
Cleaned By			Signature		
Notes					

Date		Day		Time	
Building			Location		
Cleaned By			Signature		
Notes					

Date		Day		Time	
Building			Location		
Cleaned By			Signature		
Notes					

Date		Day		Time	
Building			Location		
Cleaned By			Signature		
Notes					

Date		Day		Time	
Building			Location		
Cleaned By			Signature		
Notes					

Date		Day		Time	
Building			Location		
Cleaned By			Signature		
Notes					

Date		Day		Time	
Building			Location		
Cleaned By			Signature		
Notes					

Date		Day		Time	
Building			Location		
Cleaned By			Signature		
Notes					

Date		Day		Time	
Building			Location		
Cleaned By			Signature		
Notes					

Date		Day		Time	
Building			Location		
Cleaned By			Signature		
Notes					

Date		Day		Time	
Building			Location		
Cleaned By			Signature		
Notes					

Date		Day		Time	
Building		Location			
Cleaned By		Signature			
Notes					

Date		Day		Time	
Building		Location			
Cleaned By		Signature			
Notes					

Date		Day		Time	
Building		Location			
Cleaned By		Signature			
Notes					

Date		Day		Time	
Building		Location			
Cleaned By		Signature			
Notes					

Date		Day		Time	
Building		Location			
Cleaned By		Signature			
Notes					

Date		Day		Time	
Building		Location			
Cleaned By		Signature			
Notes					

Date		Day		Time	
Building			Location		
Cleaned By			Signature		
Notes					

Date		Day		Time	
Building			Location		
Cleaned By			Signature		
Notes					

Date		Day		Time	
Building			Location		
Cleaned By			Signature		
Notes					

Date		Day		Time	
Building			Location		
Cleaned By			Signature		
Notes					

Date		Day		Time	
Building			Location		
Cleaned By			Signature		
Notes					

Date		Day		Time	
Building			Location		
Cleaned By			Signature		
Notes					

Date		Day		Time	
Building			Location		
Cleaned By			Signature		
Notes					

Date		Day		Time	
Building			Location		
Cleaned By			Signature		
Notes					

Date		Day		Time	
Building			Location		
Cleaned By			Signature		
Notes					

Date		Day		Time	
Building			Location		
Cleaned By			Signature		
Notes					

Date		Day		Time	
Building			Location		
Cleaned By			Signature		
Notes					

Date		Day		Time	
Building			Location		
Cleaned By			Signature		
Notes					

Date		Day		Time	
Building			Location		
Cleaned By			Signature		
Notes					

Date		Day		Time	
Building			Location		
Cleaned By			Signature		
Notes					

Date		Day		Time	
Building			Location		
Cleaned By			Signature		
Notes					

Date		Day		Time	
Building			Location		
Cleaned By			Signature		
Notes					

Date		Day		Time	
Building			Location		
Cleaned By			Signature		
Notes					

Date		Day		Time	
Building			Location		
Cleaned By			Signature		
Notes					

Date		Day		Time	
Building			Location		
Cleaned By			Signature		
Notes					

Date		Day		Time	
Building			Location		
Cleaned By			Signature		
Notes					

Date		Day		Time	
Building			Location		
Cleaned By			Signature		
Notes					

Date		Day		Time	
Building			Location		
Cleaned By			Signature		
Notes					

Date		Day		Time	
Building			Location		
Cleaned By			Signature		
Notes					

Date		Day		Time	
Building			Location		
Cleaned By			Signature		
Notes					

Date		Day		Time	
Building			Location		
Cleaned By			Signature		
Notes					

Date		Day		Time	
Building			Location		
Cleaned By			Signature		
Notes					

Date		Day		Time	
Building			Location		
Cleaned By			Signature		
Notes					

Date		Day		Time	
Building			Location		
Cleaned By			Signature		
Notes					

Date		Day		Time	
Building			Location		
Cleaned By			Signature		
Notes					

Date		Day		Time	
Building			Location		
Cleaned By			Signature		
Notes					

Date		Day		Time	
Building			Location		
Cleaned By			Signature		
Notes					

Date		Day		Time	
Building			Location		
Cleaned By			Signature		
Notes					

Date		Day		Time	
Building			Location		
Cleaned By			Signature		
Notes					

Date		Day		Time	
Building			Location		
Cleaned By			Signature		
Notes					

Date		Day		Time	
Building			Location		
Cleaned By			Signature		
Notes					

Date		Day		Time	
Building			Location		
Cleaned By			Signature		
Notes					

Date		Day		Time	
Building			Location		
Cleaned By			Signature		
Notes					

Date		Day		Time	
Building			Location		
Cleaned By			Signature		
Notes					

Date		Day		Time	
Building			Location		
Cleaned By			Signature		
Notes					

Date		Day		Time	
Building			Location		
Cleaned By			Signature		
Notes					

Date		Day		Time	
Building			Location		
Cleaned By			Signature		
Notes					

Date		Day		Time	
Building			Location		
Cleaned By			Signature		
Notes					

Date		Day		Time	
Building			Location		
Cleaned By			Signature		
Notes					

Date		Day		Time	
Building			Location		
Cleaned By			Signature		
Notes					

Date		Day		Time	
Building			Location		
Cleaned By			Signature		
Notes					

Date		Day		Time	
Building			Location		
Cleaned By			Signature		
Notes					

Date		Day		Time	
Building			Location		
Cleaned By			Signature		
Notes					

Date		Day		Time	
Building			Location		
Cleaned By			Signature		
Notes					

Date		Day		Time	
Building			Location		
Cleaned By			Signature		
Notes					

Date		Day		Time	
Building			Location		
Cleaned By			Signature		
Notes					

Date		Day		Time	
Building			Location		
Cleaned By			Signature		
Notes					

Date		Day		Time	
Building			Location		
Cleaned By			Signature		
Notes					

Date		Day		Time	
Building			Location		
Cleaned By			Signature		
Notes					

Date		Day		Time	
Building			Location		
Cleaned By			Signature		
Notes					

Date		Day		Time	
Building			Location		
Cleaned By			Signature		
Notes					

Date		Day		Time	
Building			Location		
Cleaned By			Signature		
Notes					

Date		Day		Time	
Building			Location		
Cleaned By			Signature		
Notes					

Date		Day		Time	
Building			Location		
Cleaned By			Signature		
Notes					

Date		Day		Time	
Building			Location		
Cleaned By			Signature		
Notes					

Date		Day		Time	
Building			Location		
Cleaned By			Signature		
Notes					

FOOD WASTE LOG

Week : _____ Month : _____ Facility : _____

Date	Time	Item Description	Reason For Waste	Quantity	Cost Per Unit	Total Cost	Checked By	Initials

Week : _____ Month : _____ Facility : _____

Date	Time	Item Description	Reason For Waste	Quantity	Cost Per Unit	Total Cost	Checked By	Initials

Week : _____ Month : _____ Facility : _____

Date	Time	Item Description	Reason For Waste	Quantity	Cost Per Unit	Total Cost	Checked By	Initials

Week : _____   Month : _____   Facility : _____

Date	Time	Item Description	Reason For Waste	Quantity	Cost Per Unit	Total Cost	Checked By	Initials

Week : _____ Month : _____ Facility : _____

Date	Time	Item Description	Reason For Waste	Quantity	Cost Per Unit	Total Cost	Checked By	Initials

Week : _____ Month : _____ Facility : _____

Date	Time	Item Description	Reason For Waste	Quantity	Cost Per Unit	Total Cost	Checked By	Initials

Week : _____ Month : _____ Facility : _____

Date	Time	Item Description	Reason For Waste	Quantity	Cost Per Unit	Total Cost	Checked By	Initials

Week : _____ Month : _____ Facility : _____

Date	Time	Item Description	Reason For Waste	Quantity	Cost Per Unit	Total Cost	Checked By	Initials

Week : _____ Month : _____ Facility : _____

Date	Time	Item Description	Reason For Waste	Quantity	Cost Per Unit	Total Cost	Checked By	Initials

Week : _____ Month : _____ Facility : _____

Date	Time	Item Description	Reason For Waste	Quantity	Cost Per Unit	Total Cost	Checked By	Initials

Week : _____ Month : _____ Facility : _____

Date	Time	Item Description	Reason For Waste	Quantity	Cost Per Unit	Total Cost	Checked By	Initials

Week : _____ Month : _____ Facility : _____

Date	Time	Item Description	Reason For Waste	Quantity	Cost Per Unit	Total Cost	Checked By	Initials

Week : _____ Month : _____ Facility : _____

Date	Time	Item Description	Reason For Waste	Quantity	Cost Per Unit	Total Cost	Checked By	Initials

Week : _____ Month : _____ Facility : _____

Date	Time	Item Description	Reason For Waste	Quantity	Cost Per Unit	Total Cost	Checked By	Initials

Week : _____ Month : _____ Facility : _____

Date	Time	Item Description	Reason For Waste	Quantity	Cost Per Unit	Total Cost	Checked By	Initials

Week : _____ Month : _____ Facility : _____

Date	Time	Item Description	Reason For Waste	Quantity	Cost Per Unit	Total Cost	Checked By	Initials

Week : _____ Month : _____ Facility : _____

Date	Time	Item Description	Reason For Waste	Quantity	Cost Per Unit	Total Cost	Checked By	Initials

Week : _____ Month : _____ Facility : _____

Date	Time	Item Description	Reason For Waste	Quantity	Cost Per Unit	Total Cost	Checked By	Initials

Week : _____ Month : _____ Facility : _____

Date	Time	Item Description	Reason For Waste	Quantity	Cost Per Unit	Total Cost	Checked By	Initials

Week : _____ Month : _____ Facility : _____

Date	Time	Item Description	Reason For Waste	Quantity	Cost Per Unit	Total Cost	Checked By	Initials

Week : _____ Month : _____ Facility : _____

Date	Time	Item Description	Reason For Waste	Quantity	Cost Per Unit	Total Cost	Checked By	Initials

Week : _____ Month : _____ Facility : _____

Date	Time	Item Description	Reason For Waste	Quantity	Cost Per Unit	Total Cost	Checked By	Initials

Week : _____ Month : _____ Facility : _____

Date	Time	Item Description	Reason For Waste	Quantity	Cost Per Unit	Total Cost	Checked By	Initials

Week : _____ Month : _____ Facility : _____

Date	Time	Item Description	Reason For Waste	Quantity	Cost Per Unit	Total Cost	Checked By	Initials

Week : _____ Month : _____ Facility : _____

Date	Time	Item Description	Reason For Waste	Quantity	Cost Per Unit	Total Cost	Checked By	Initials

Week : _____ Month : _____ Facility : _____

Date	Time	Item Description	Reason For Waste	Quantity	Cost Per Unit	Total Cost	Checked By	Initials

Week : _____ Month : _____ Facility : _____

Date	Time	Item Description	Reason For Waste	Quantity	Cost Per Unit	Total Cost	Checked By	Initials

Week : _____ Month : _____ Facility : _____

Date	Time	Item Description	Reason For Waste	Quantity	Cost Per Unit	Total Cost	Checked By	Initials

Week : _____ Month : _____ Facility : _____

Date	Time	Item Description	Reason For Waste	Quantity	Cost Per Unit	Total Cost	Checked By	Initials

Week : _____ Month : _____ Facility : _____

Date	Time	Item Description	Reason For Waste	Quantity	Cost Per Unit	Total Cost	Checked By	Initials

Week : _____ Month : _____ Facility : _____

Date	Time	Item Description	Reason For Waste	Quantity	Cost Per Unit	Total Cost	Checked By	Initials

Week : _____ Month : _____ Facility : _____

Date	Time	Item Description	Reason For Waste	Quantity	Cost Per Unit	Total Cost	Checked By	Initials

Week : _____ Month : _____ Facility : _____

Date	Time	Item Description	Reason For Waste	Quantity	Cost Per Unit	Total Cost	Checked By	Initials

Week : _____ Month : _____ Facility : _____

Date	Time	Item Description	Reason For Waste	Quantity	Cost Per Unit	Total Cost	Checked By	Initials

Week : _____ Month : _____ Facility : _____

Date	Time	Item Description	Reason For Waste	Quantity	Cost Per Unit	Total Cost	Checked By	Initials

Week : _____ Month : _____ Facility : _____

Date	Time	Item Description	Reason For Waste	Quantity	Cost Per Unit	Total Cost	Checked By	Initials

Week : _____ Month : _____ Facility : _____

Date	Time	Item Description	Reason For Waste	Quantity	Cost Per Unit	Total Cost	Checked By	Initials

Week : _____ Month : _____ Facility : _____

Date	Time	Item Description	Reason For Waste	Quantity	Cost Per Unit	Total Cost	Checked By	Initials

Printed in Great Britain
by Amazon

83193959R00072